T0084263

2ND EDITION

ISBN 978-1-70518-854-5

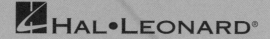

Visit Hal Leonard Online at
www.halleonard.com

World headquarters, contact:
Hal Leonard
7777 West Bluemound Road
Milwaukee, WI 53213
Email: info@halleonard.com

In Europe, contact:
Hal Leonard Europe Limited
1 Red Place
London, W1K 6PL
Email: info@halleonardeurope.com

In Australia, contact:
Hal Leonard Australia Pty. Ltd.
4 Lentara Court
Cheltenham, Victoria, 3192 Australia
Email: info@halleonard.com.au

Beauty and the Beast
from BEAUTY AND THE BEAST

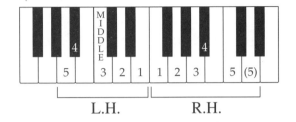

Music by Alan Menken
Lyrics by Howard Ashman

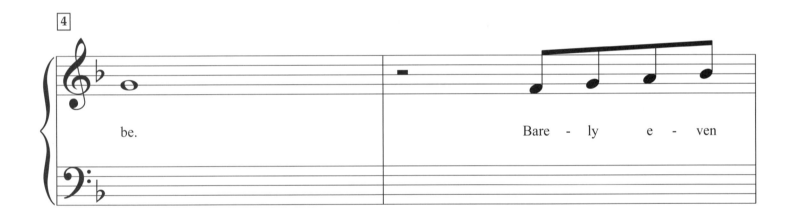

Duet Part (Student plays one octave higher than written.)
With expression

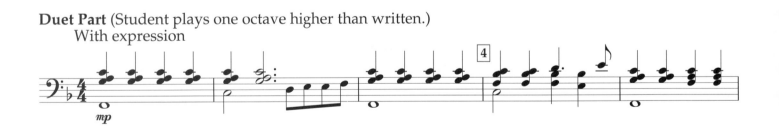

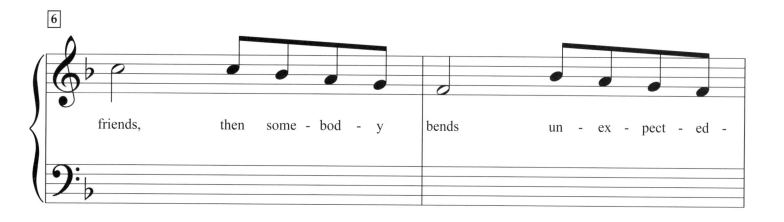

friends,   then   some - bod - y   bends   un - ex - pect - ed -

ly.   Just a lit - tle   change,

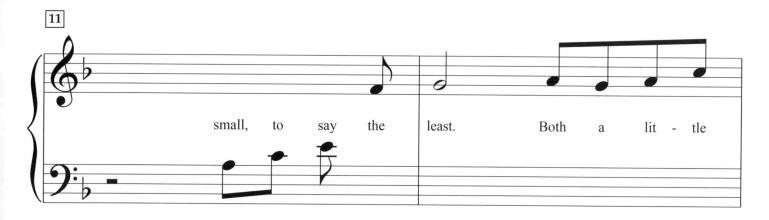

small, to say the   least.   Both   a   lit - tle

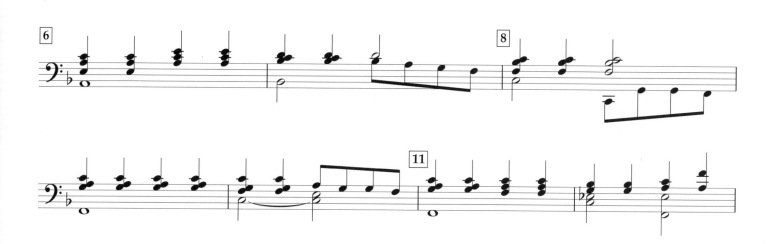

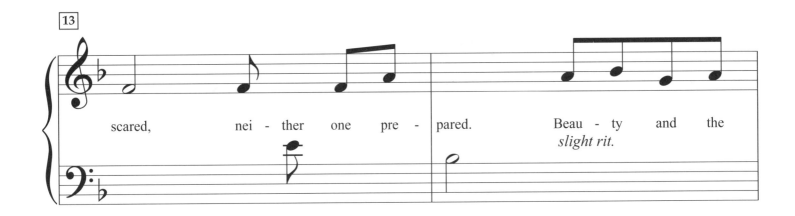

scared,　nei - ther　one　pre - pared.　Beau - ty　and　the
slight rit.

Beast.
a tempo

Ev - er　just　the　same.

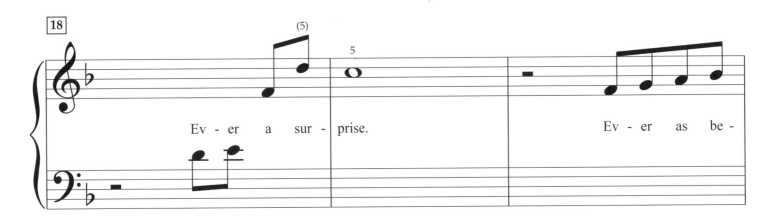

Ev - er　a　sur - prise.

Ev - er　as　be -

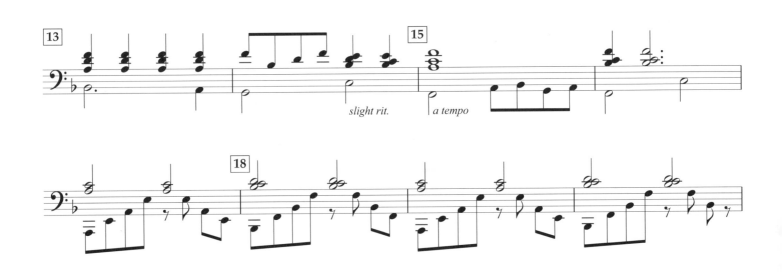

slight rit.　*a tempo*

4

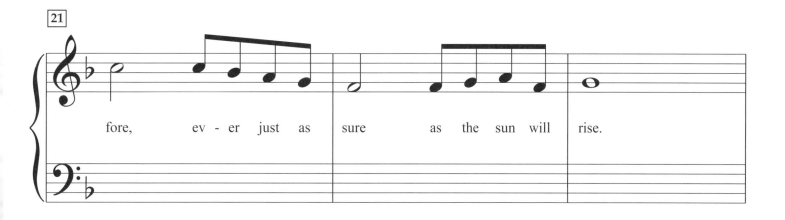

fore,   ev - er   just   as   sure   as   the   sun   will   rise.

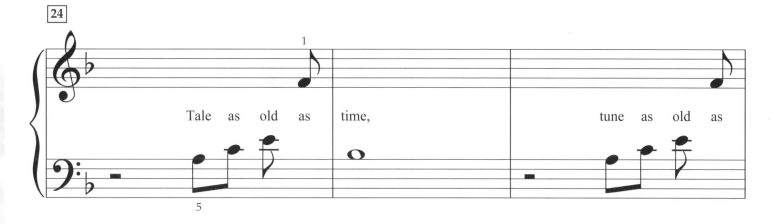

Tale   as   old   as   time,   tune   as   old   as

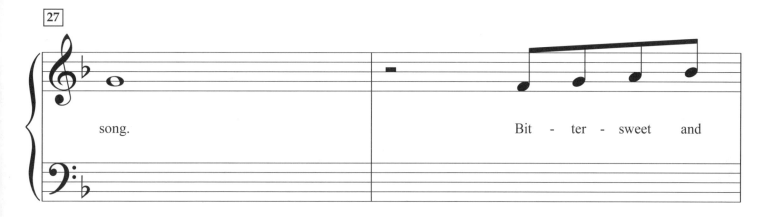

song.   Bit   -   ter - sweet   and

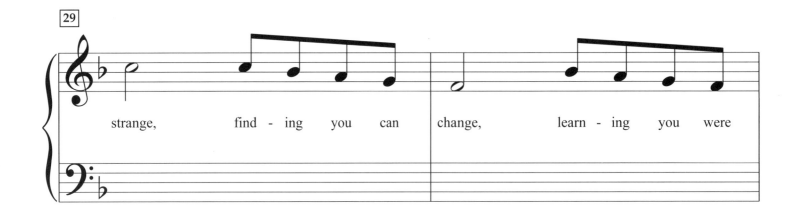

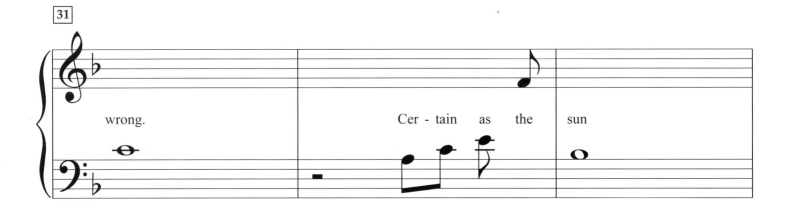

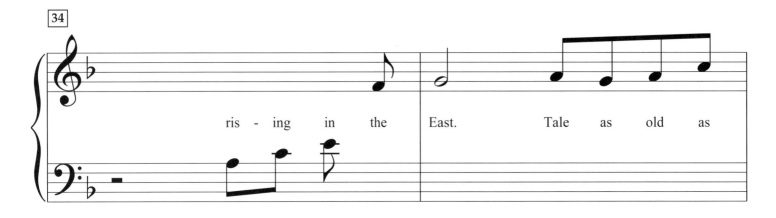

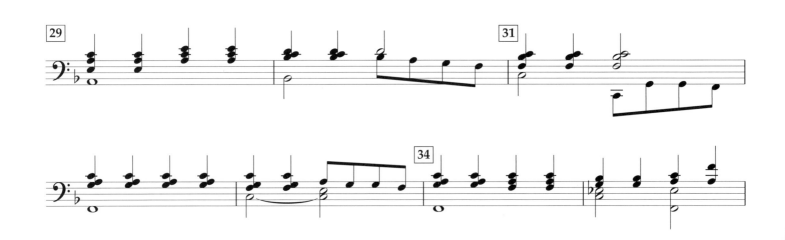

6

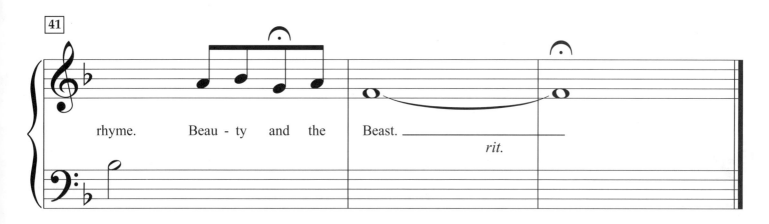

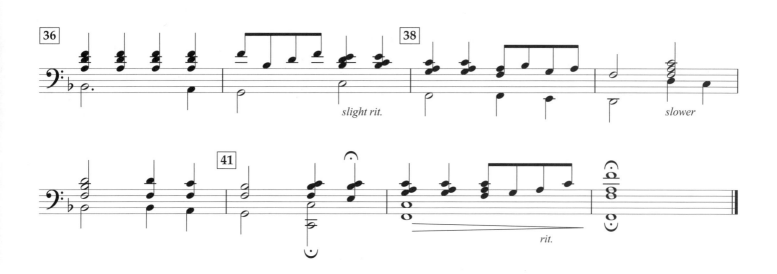

7

Candle on the Water
from PETE'S DRAGON

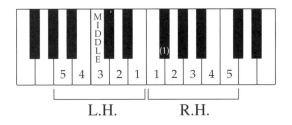

Words and Music by Al Kasha
and Joel Hirschhorn

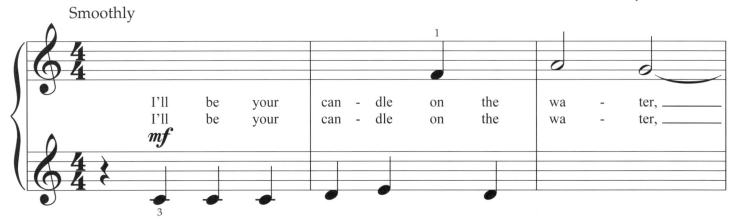

I'll be your can - dle on the wa - ter, _____
I'll be your can - dle on the wa - ter, _____

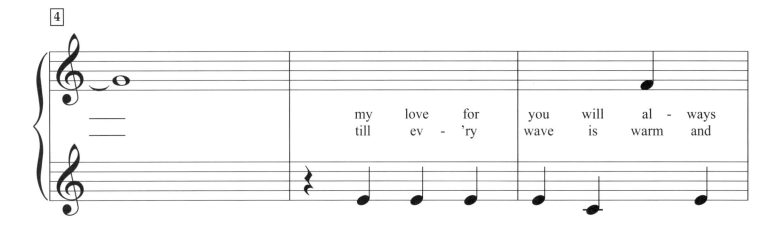

_____ my love for you will al - ways
_____ till ev - 'ry wave is warm and

Duet Part (Student plays one octave higher than written.)
Smoothly

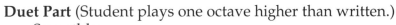

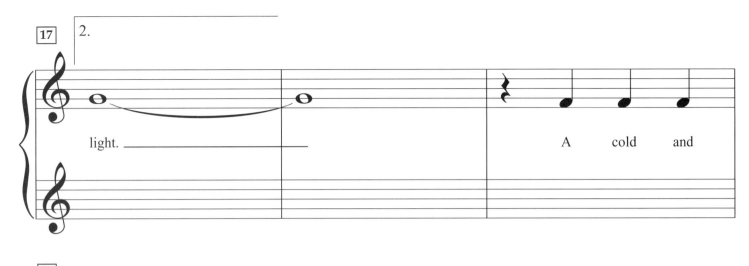

light. _____

A cold and

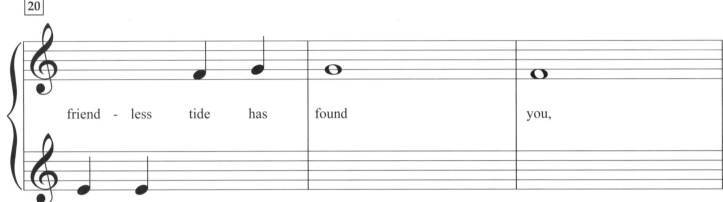

friend - less tide has found you,

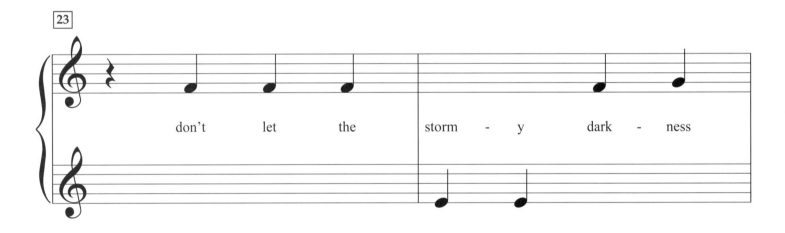

don't let the storm - y dark - ness

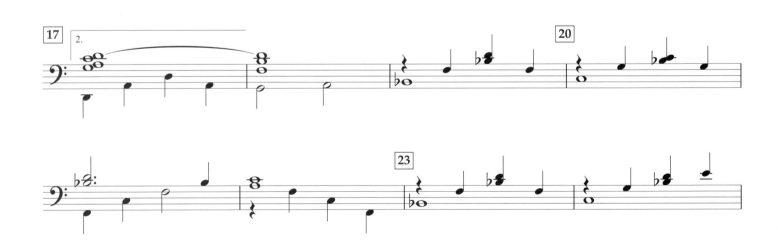

pull   you   down.   I'll   paint   a

ray   of   hope   a - round   you,

cir - cling   in   the   air,   light - ed   by   a

11

let   you   go. _____

I'll   nev - er   let   you   go. _____

15

Ever Ever After

from ENCHANTED

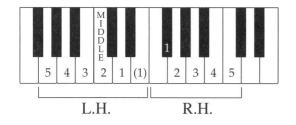

Music by Alan Menken
Lyrics by Stephen Schwartz

Happily

Sto - ry - book end - ings, fair - y tales com - ing true; ___
Start a new fash - ion: wear your heart on your sleeve.

4

deep down in - side, we wan - na be - lieve ___ they still
Some - times you reach what's real just by mak - ing be -

Duet Part (Student plays one octave higher than written.)

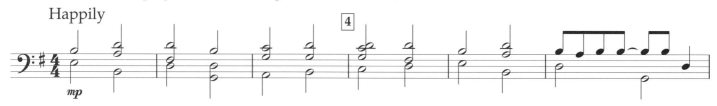

Happily

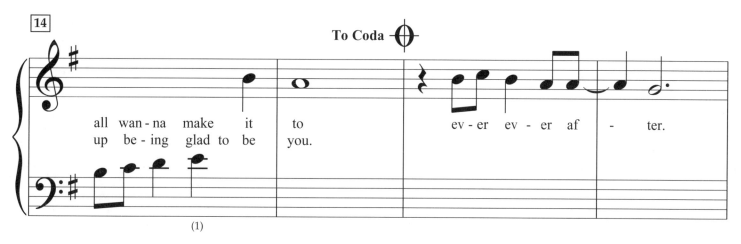

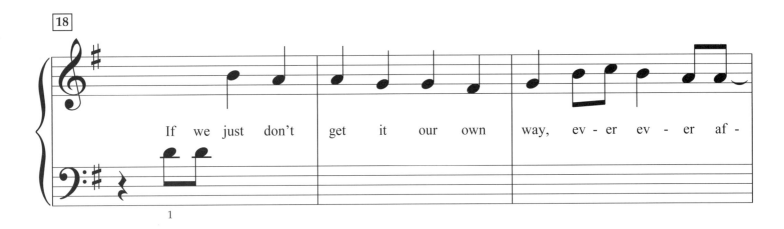

If we just don't get it our own way, ev - er ev - er af-

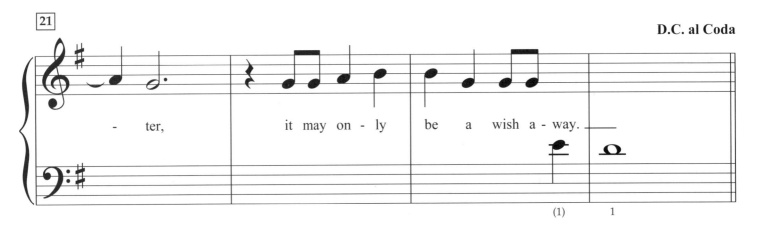

D.C. al Coda

- ter, it may on - ly be a wish a - way.

CODA

Ev - er ev - er af - ter; though the world will tell

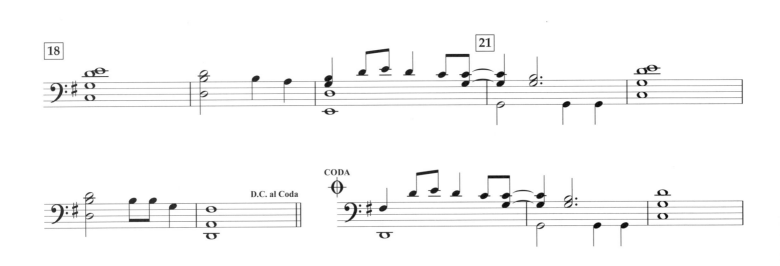

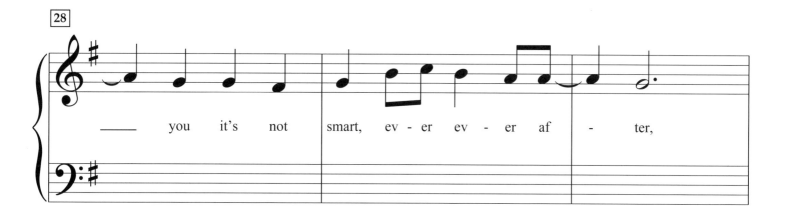

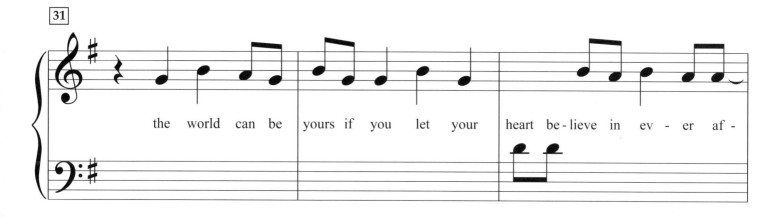

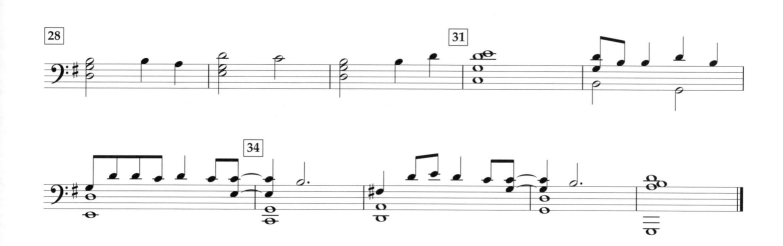

The Family Madrigal

from ENCANTO

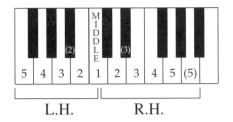

Music and Lyrics by
Lin-Manuel Miranda

With a Latin groove

This is our home, we've got ev - 'ry gen - er - a - tion.

So full of mu - sic, a rhy-thm of its own de-sign. This is my fam - 'ly, a

Duet Part (Student plays one octave higher than written.)

With a Latin groove

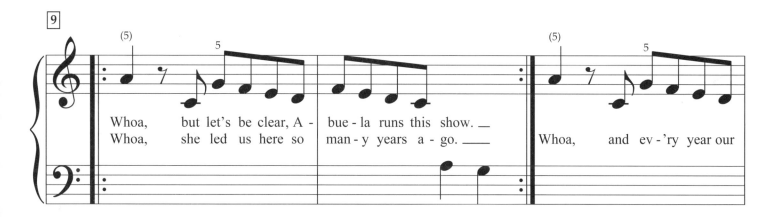

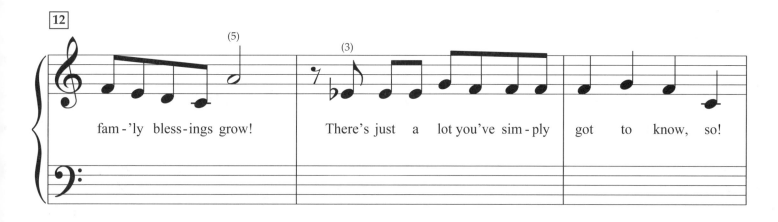

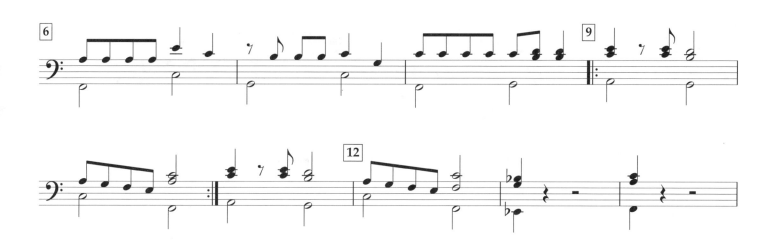

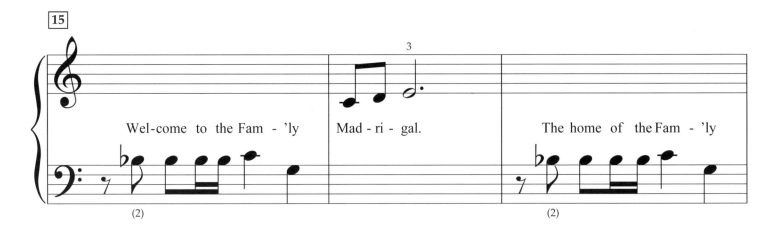

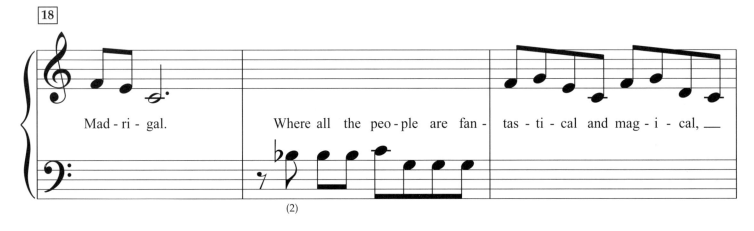

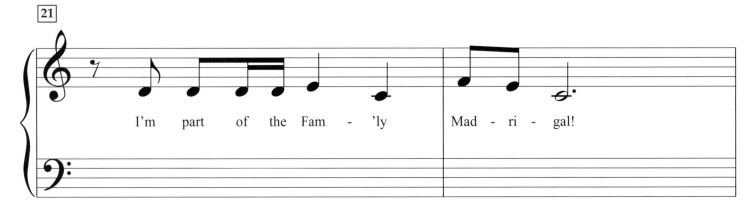

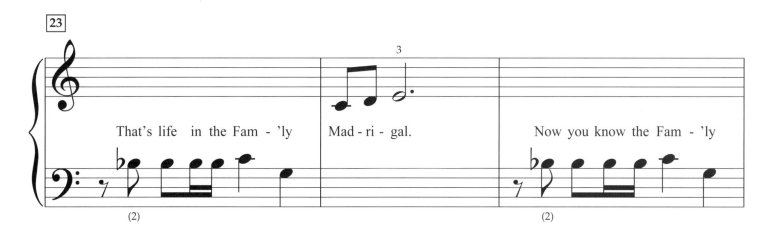

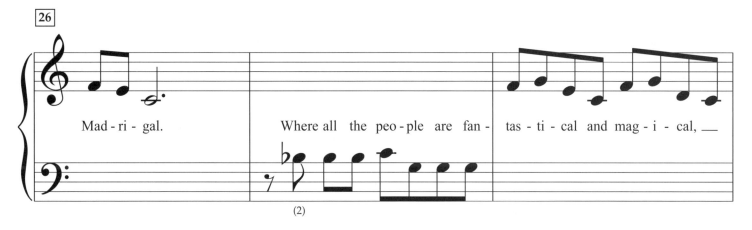

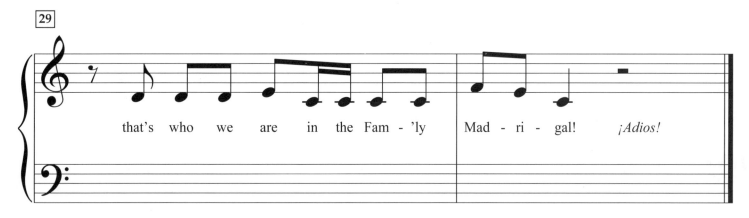

Lost in the Woods
from FROZEN 2

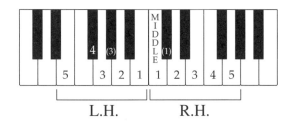

L.H.   R.H.

Music and Lyrics by Kristen Anderson-Lopez
and Robert Lopez

Moderately, in 2

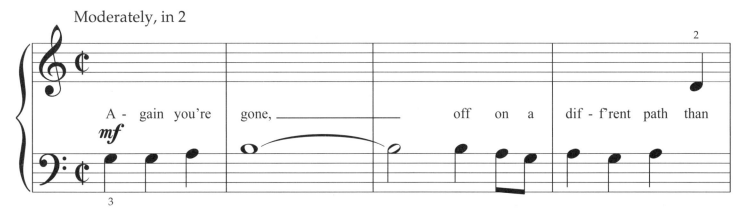

A - gain you're gone, off on a dif - f'rent path than

mine, I'm left be - hind, won-der-ing if I should fol - low.

Duet Part (Student plays one octave higher than written.)

Moderately, in 2

You had to go, _____ and of course it's al - ways

fine. I prob - 'ly could catch up with you to - mor - row. _____

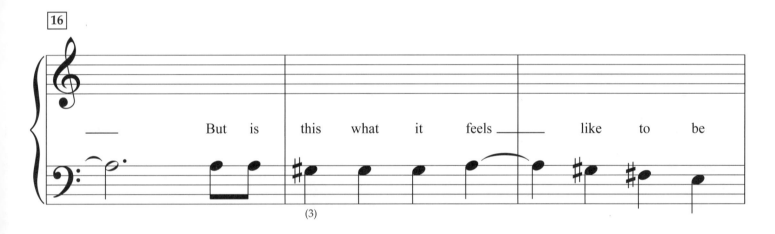

_____ But is this what it feels _____ like to be

(3)

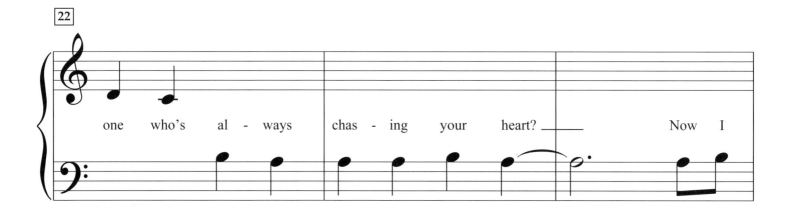

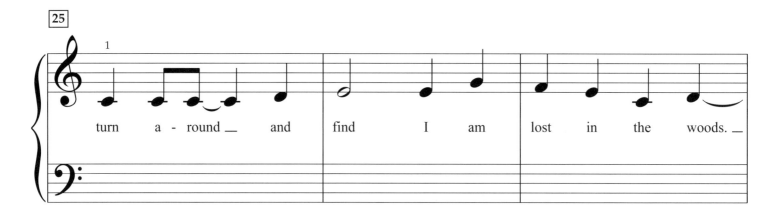

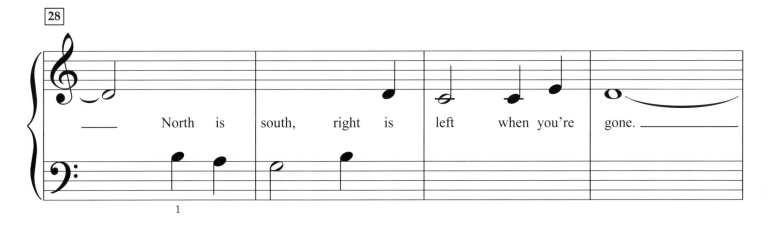

North is south, right is left when you're gone.

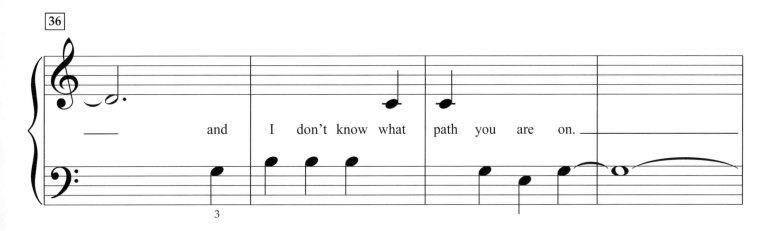

I'm the one who sees you home, but now I'm lost in the woods,

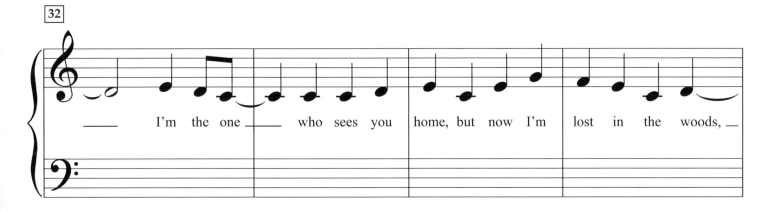

and I don't know what path you are on.

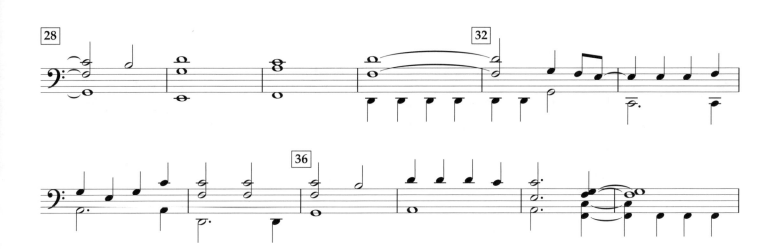

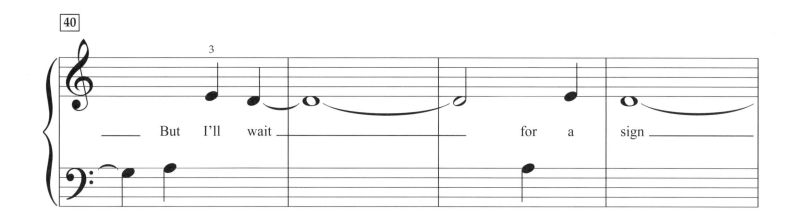

But I'll wait _____ for a sign _____

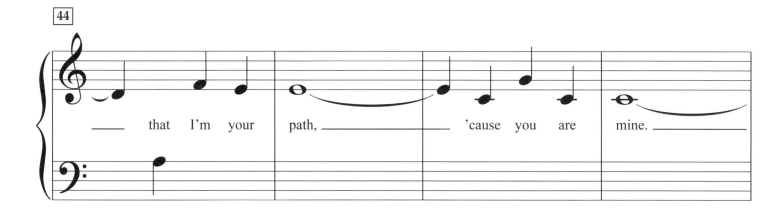

_____ that I'm your path, _____ 'cause you are mine. _____

_____ Un-til then, I'm lost in the woods.

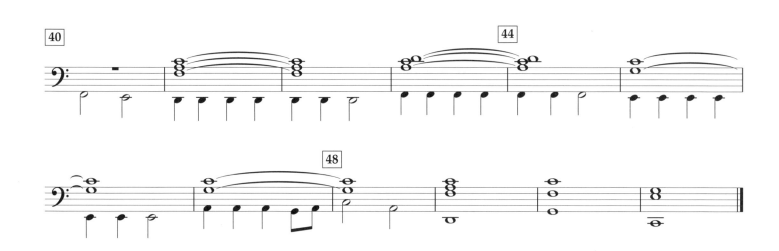

Proud Corazón
from Coco

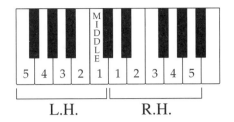

Music by Germaine Franco
Lyrics by Adrian Molina

Quickly

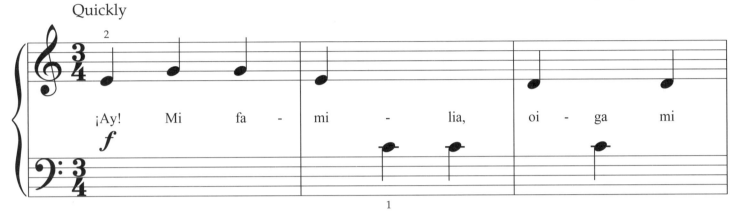

¡Ay! Mi fa - mi - lia, oi - ga mi gen - te. Can - ten a co - ro.

Duet Part (Student plays one octave higher than written.)

Quickly

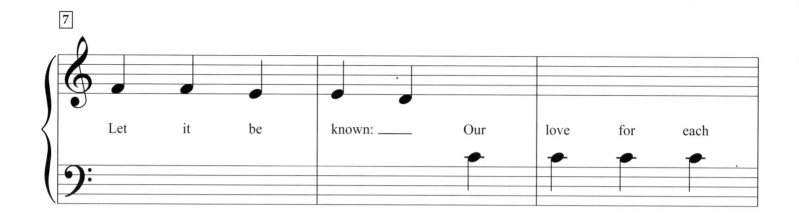

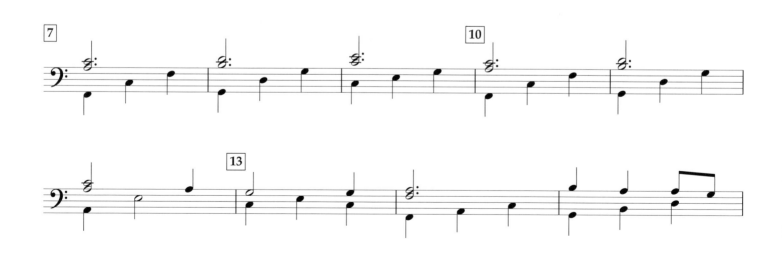

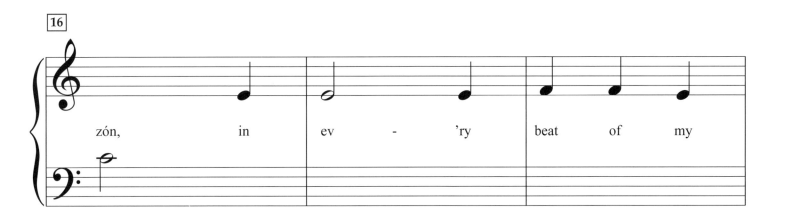

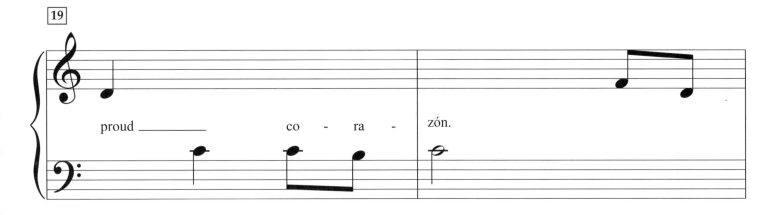

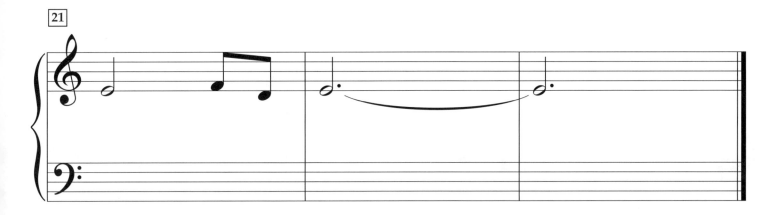

Loyal Brave True
from MULAN (2020)

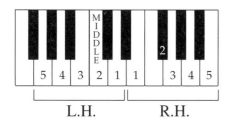

Written by Jamie Hartman,
Billy Crabtree, Rosi Golan
and Harry Gregson-Williams

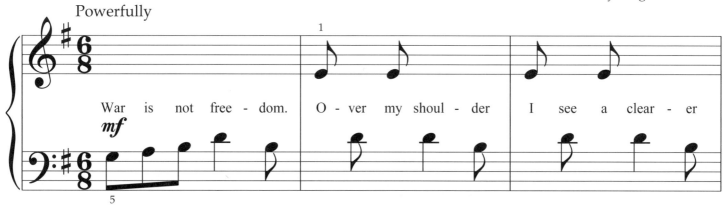

Duet Part (Student plays one octave higher than written.)

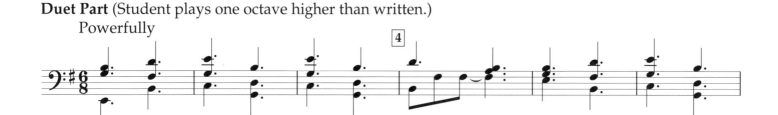

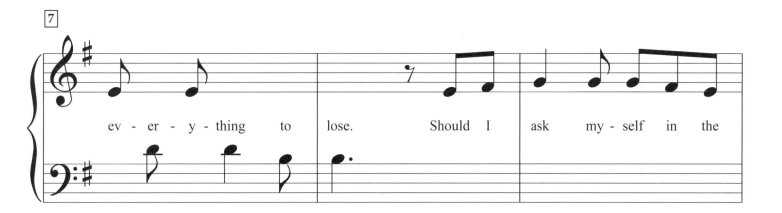

ev - er - y - thing to lose. Should I ask my - self in the

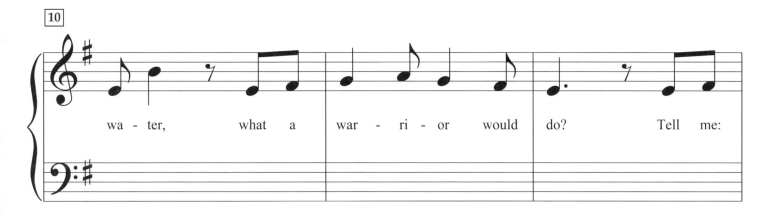

wa - ter, what a war - ri - or would do? Tell me:

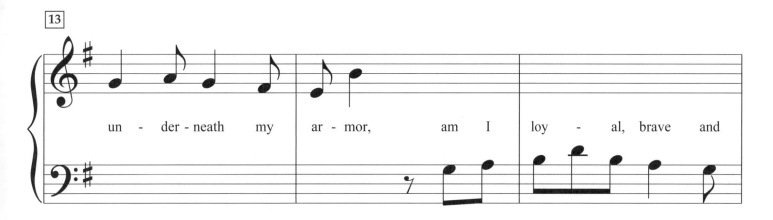

un - der - neath my ar - mor, am I loy - al, brave and

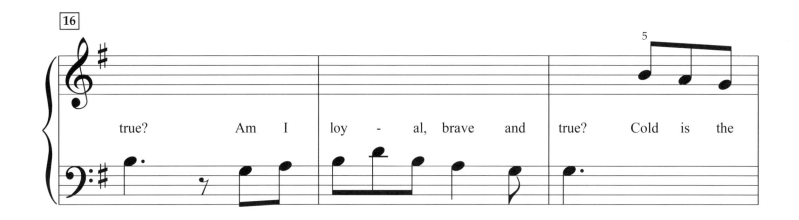

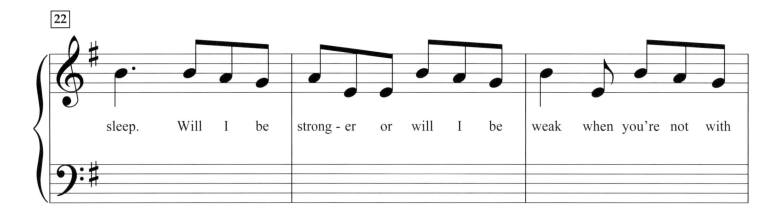

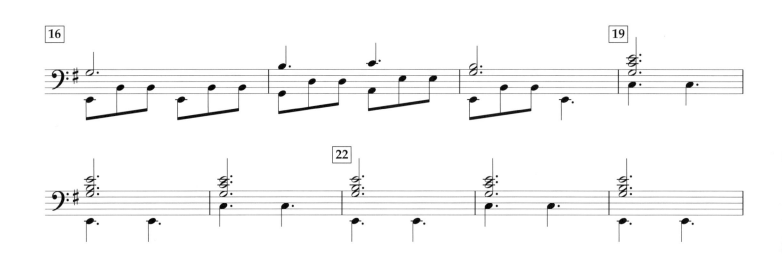

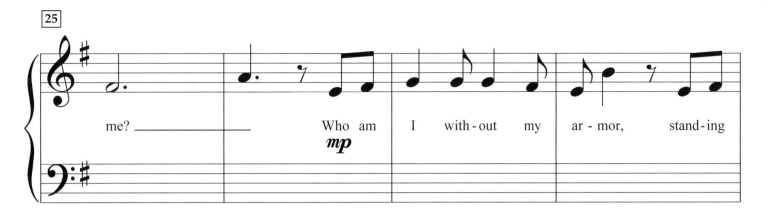

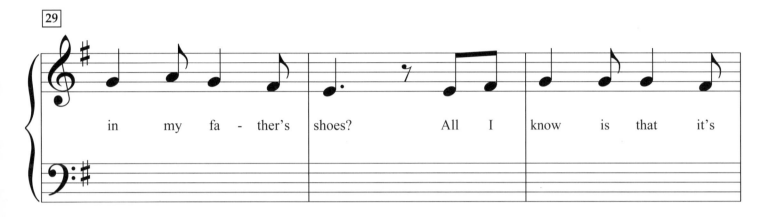

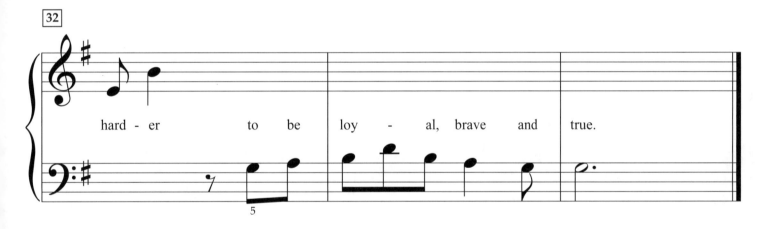

Speechless
from ALADDIN (2019)

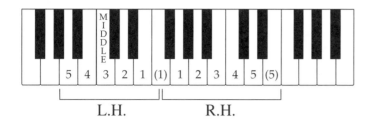

Music by Alan Menken
Lyrics by Benj Pasek and Justin Paul

Moving along

Here comes a wave meant to wash me a-way, a tide that is tak-ing me

un - der. Swal-low-ing sand, left with noth-ing to say, my

Duet Part (Student plays one octave higher than written.)

Moving along

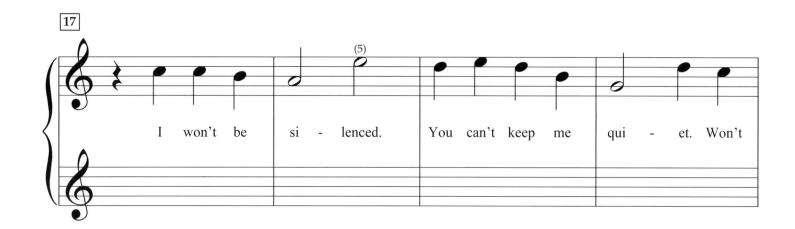

I won't be si - lenced. You can't keep me qui - et. Won't

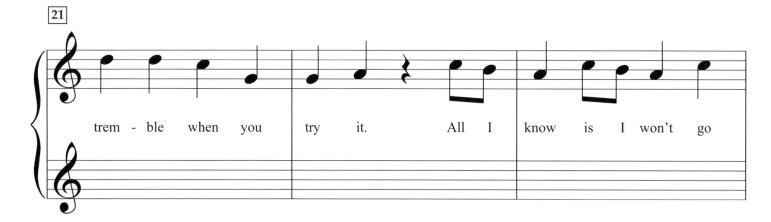

trem - ble when you try it. All I know is I won't go

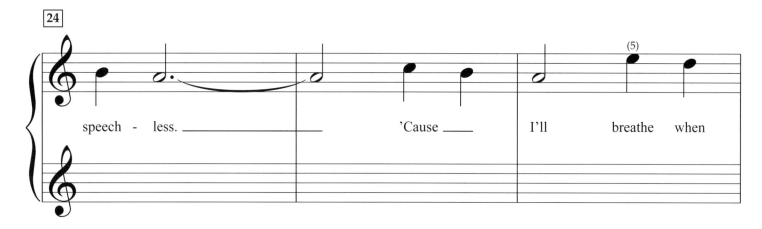

speech - less. _____ 'Cause ____ I'll breathe when

38

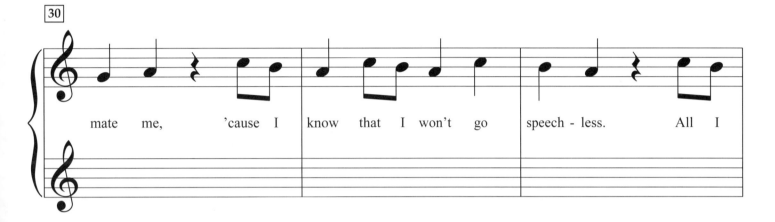

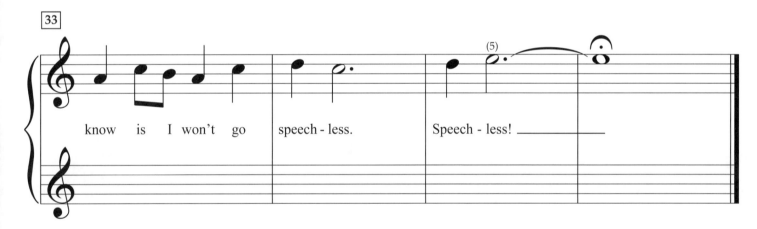

Surface Pressure
from ENCANTO

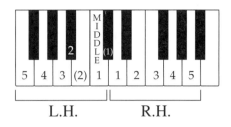

L.H.   R.H.

Music and Lyrics by
Lin-Manuel Miranda

Moderately fast

mf Un - der the sur - face, I feel ber - serk as a tight - rope walk - er in a

three - ring cir - cus. Un - der the sur - face, was Her - cu - les

Duet Part (Student plays one octave higher than written.)

Moderately fast

mp

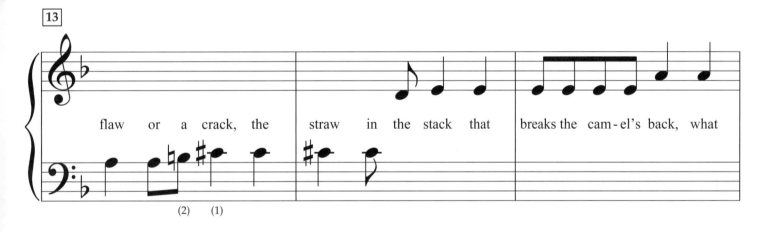

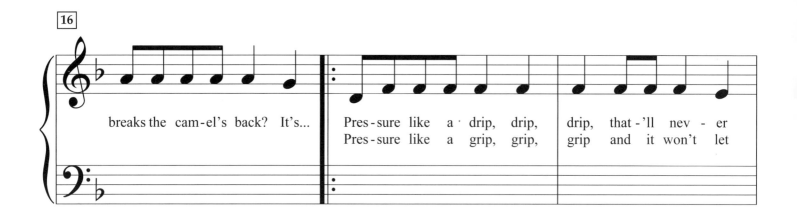

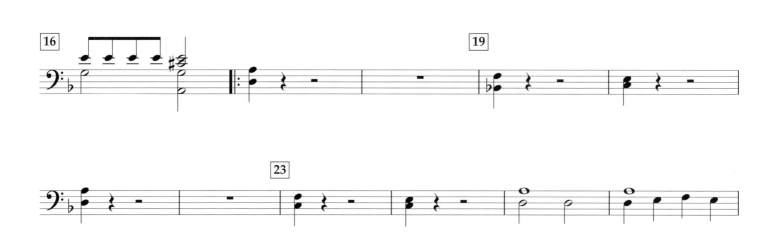

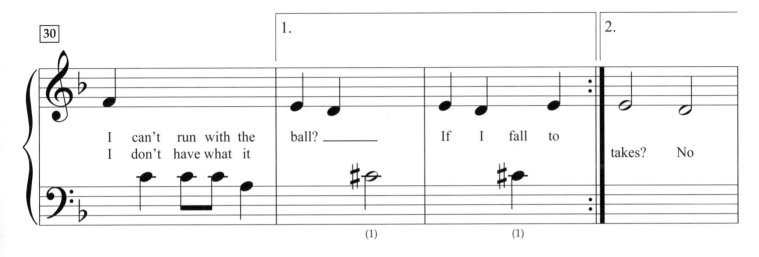

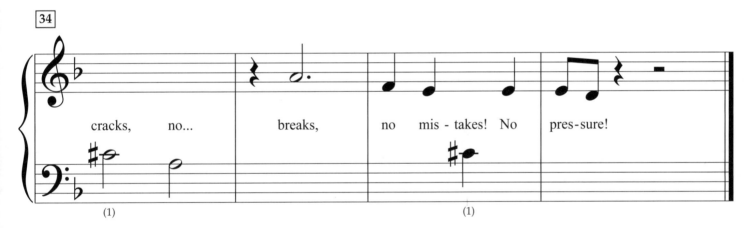

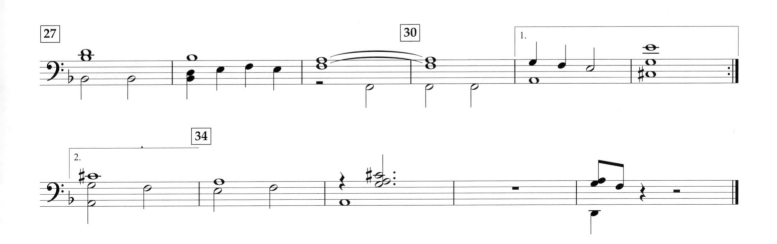

We Don't Talk About Bruno
from ENCANTO

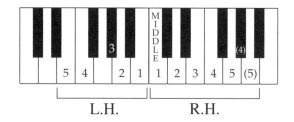

Music and Lyrics by
Lin-Manuel Miranda

Duet Part (Student plays one octave higher than written.)

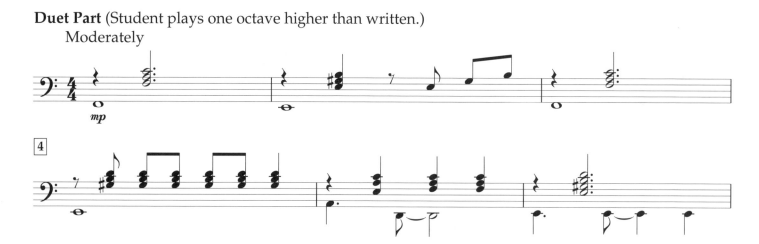

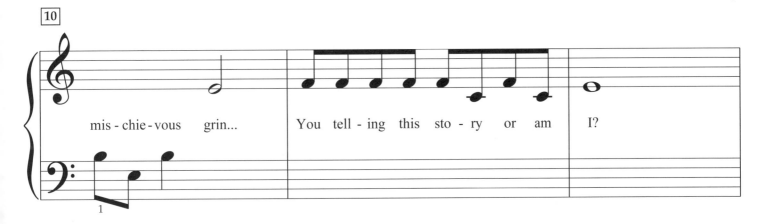

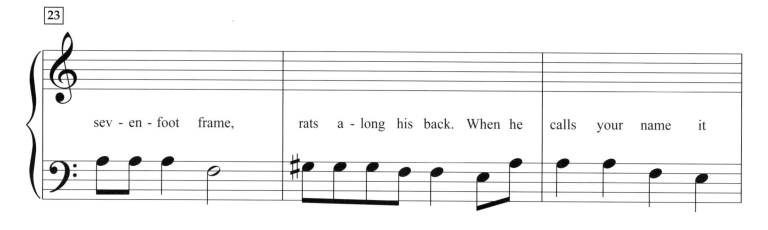

PLAYING PIANO HAS NEVER BEEN EASIER!

Five-Finger Piano songbooks from Hal Leonard are designed for students in their first year of study. They feature single-note melody lines that stay in one position, indicated by a small keyboard diagram at the beginning of each song. Each song also includes lyrics, and beautifully written piano accompaniments that can be played by teachers, parents or more experienced students to give new players a "it sounds so good!" experience.

    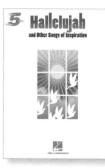 

Adele
00175097 8 songs $9.99

Beatles! Beatles!
00292061 8 songs $8.99

Beatles Favorites
00310369 8 songs $10.99

The Beatles Hits
00128687 8 songs $8.99

Cartoon Fun
00279151 8 songs $8.99

A Charlie Brown Christmas™
00316069 10 songs $10.99

The Charlie Brown Collection™
00316072 8 songs $8.99

Children's TV Favorites
00311208 8 songs $7.95

Christmas Carols
00236800 10 songs $7.99

Christmas Songs Made Easy
00172307 10 songs $10.99

Church Songs for Kids
00310613 15 songs $9.99

Classical Favorites
00310611 12 selections................... $8.99

Classical Themes
00310469 10 songs $7.95

Disney Classics
00311429 7 songs $8.99

Disney Delights
00310195 9 songs $8.99

Disney Favorites
00311038 8 songs $10.99

Disney Latest Movie Hits
00277255 8 songs $10.99

Disney Movie Classics
00123475 8 songs $10.99

Disney Songs
00283429 8 songs $9.99

Disney Today
00175218 8 songs $10.99

Disney Tunes
00310375 8 songs $9.99

Disney's Princess Collection
00310847 7 songs $12.99

Eensy Weensy Spider & Other Nursery Rhyme Favorites
00310465 11 songs $7.95

First Pop Songs
00123296 8 songs $9.99

Frozen
00130374 7 songs $14.99

Frozen 2
00329705 8 songs $10.99

Fun Songs
00346769 8 songs $8.99

Hallelujah and Other Songs of Inspiration
00119649 9 songs $7.99

Happy Birthday to You and Other Great Songs
00102097 10 songs $7.99

Irish Songs
00312078 9 songs $6.99

The Lion King
00292062 5 songs $12.99

Modern Movie Favorites
00242674 8 songs $10.99

Movie Hits
00338187 8 songs $9.99

My First Hymn Book
00311873 12 songs $9.99

Over the Rainbow and Other Great Songs
00102098 10 songs $7.99

Pirates of the Caribbean
00123473 8 songs $14.99

Pop Hits
00123295 8 songs $9.99

Pop Super Hits
00311209 8 songs $7.95

Praise & Worship
00311044 8 songs $7.95

The Sound of Music
00310249 8 songs $12.99

Star Wars
00322185 10 songs $12.99

Star Wars: A Musical Journey
00322311 15 songs $16.99

Star Wars: Selections
00321903 9 songs $12.99

Today's Hits
00277909 8 songs $9.99

The Very Best of Broadway
00311039 8 songs $7.95

HAL•LEONARD®

View songlists and order online from your favorite music retailer at
halleonard.com

Disney characters & artwork TM & © 2021 Disney

Prices, contents and availability are subject to change without notice.

0323
358